FEB 03 2011
W9-AVT-054

Mars

by

Melanie Chrismer

New Lenox
Public Library District
120 Veterans Parkway
New Lenox, Illinois 60451

Children's Press
An Imprint of Scholastic Inc.
New York Toronto London Auckland Sydney
Mexico City New Delhi Hong Kong
Danbury, Connecticut

3 1984 00292 5962

These content vocabulary word builders
are for grades 1–2.

Consultant: Michelle Yehling, Astronomy Education Consultant

Photo Credits:

Photographs © 2008: Corbis Images/Roger Ressmeyer: 4 top, 5 bottom left, 5 top left, 10, 13, 17; Getty Images: 5 bottom right, 6 (Ryan McVay), 4 bottom right, 9 (Antonio M. Rosario); NASA: cover (via SODA), back cover, 1, 4 bottom left, 5 top right, 11, 15, 23 right; Photo Researchers, NY: 7 (Rev. Ronald Royer), 2, 19 (Detlev van Ravenswaay); PhotoDisc/via SODA: 23 left.

Illustration Credit:

Illustration pages 20–21 by Greg Harris

Book Design: Simonsays Design!
Book Production: The Design Lab

Library of Congress Cataloging-in-Publication Data
Chrismer, Melanie.
Mars / by Melanie Chrismer.—Updated ed.
p. cm.—(Scholastic news nonfiction readers)
Includes bibliographical references and index.
ISBN-13: 978-0-531-14697-2 (lib. bdg.) 978-0-531-14762-7 (pbk.)
ISBN-10: 0-531-14697-9 (lib. bdg.) 0-531-14762-2 (pbk.)
1. Mars (Planet)—Juvenile literature. I. Title.
QB641.C52 2007
523.43—dc22 2006102769

No part of this publication may be reproduced in whole or in part, or stored in a retrieval system, or transmitted in any form or by any means, electronic, mechanical, photocopying, recording, or otherwise, without written permission of the publisher. For information regarding permission, write to Scholastic Inc., 557 Broadway, New York, NY 10012.

Copyright © 2008, 2005 Scholastic Inc.

All rights reserved. Published by Children's Press, an imprint of Scholastic Inc.
Published simultaneously in Canada. Printed in the United States of America. 44

SCHOLASTIC, CHILDREN'S PRESS, and associated logos are trademarks and/or registered trademarks of Scholastic Inc.

1 2 3 4 5 6 7 8 9 10 R 17 16 15 14 13 12 11 10 09 08

CONTENTS

Look for these words as you read. They will be in **bold**.

astronaut
(**ass**-truh-nawt)

rover
(**roh**-ver)

solar system
(**soh**-lur **siss**-tuhm

astronomer
(uh-**stron**-uh-mur)

Mars
(mars)

space suit
(spayss soot)

telescope
(**tel**-uh-skope)

There is a bright object in the night sky that is not a star.

It is the planet **Mars**!

You can see Mars without a **telescope**.

telescope

Mars

Stars are not the only bright objects in the night sky.

Mars is the fourth planet from the Sun.

The planets in our **solar system** travel around the Sun.

Mars is sometimes called the Red Planet because of its red soil.

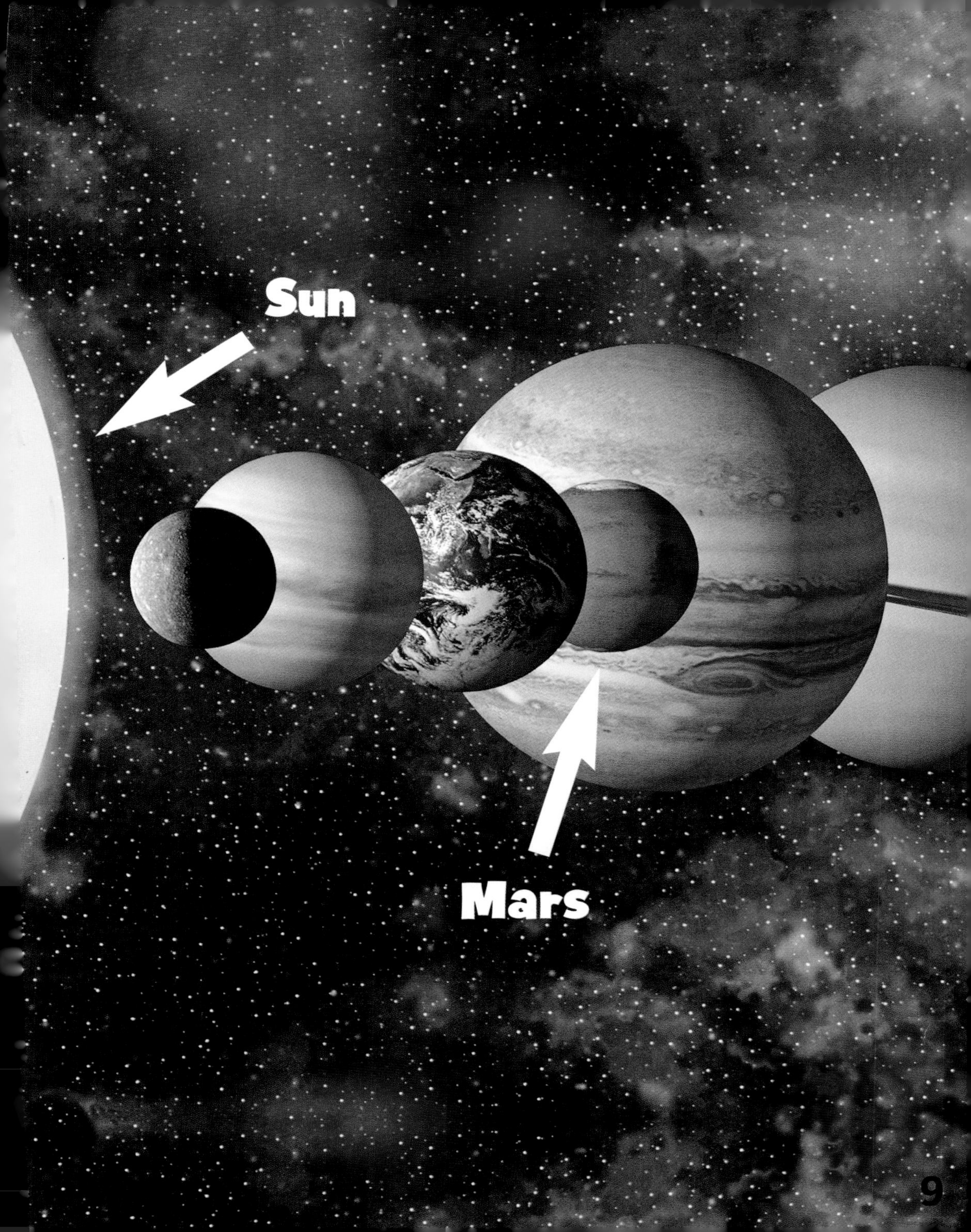
Sun
Mars

No person has gone to Mars.

Rovers have been put on Mars to explore it.

One day an **astronaut** may go to Mars.

This rover sets out to explore a rock on Mars.

An **astronomer** is someone who studies stars, planets, and space.

Astronomers use telescopes and spacecraft to study Mars.

They are studying how people might live there one day.

We could fly to Mars in a spacecraft. It would take about eight months to get there!

Computers help astronomers gather information about space.

Mars has a North Pole and a South Pole, just like Earth.

There are giant sandstorms on Mars.

Mars has two moons.

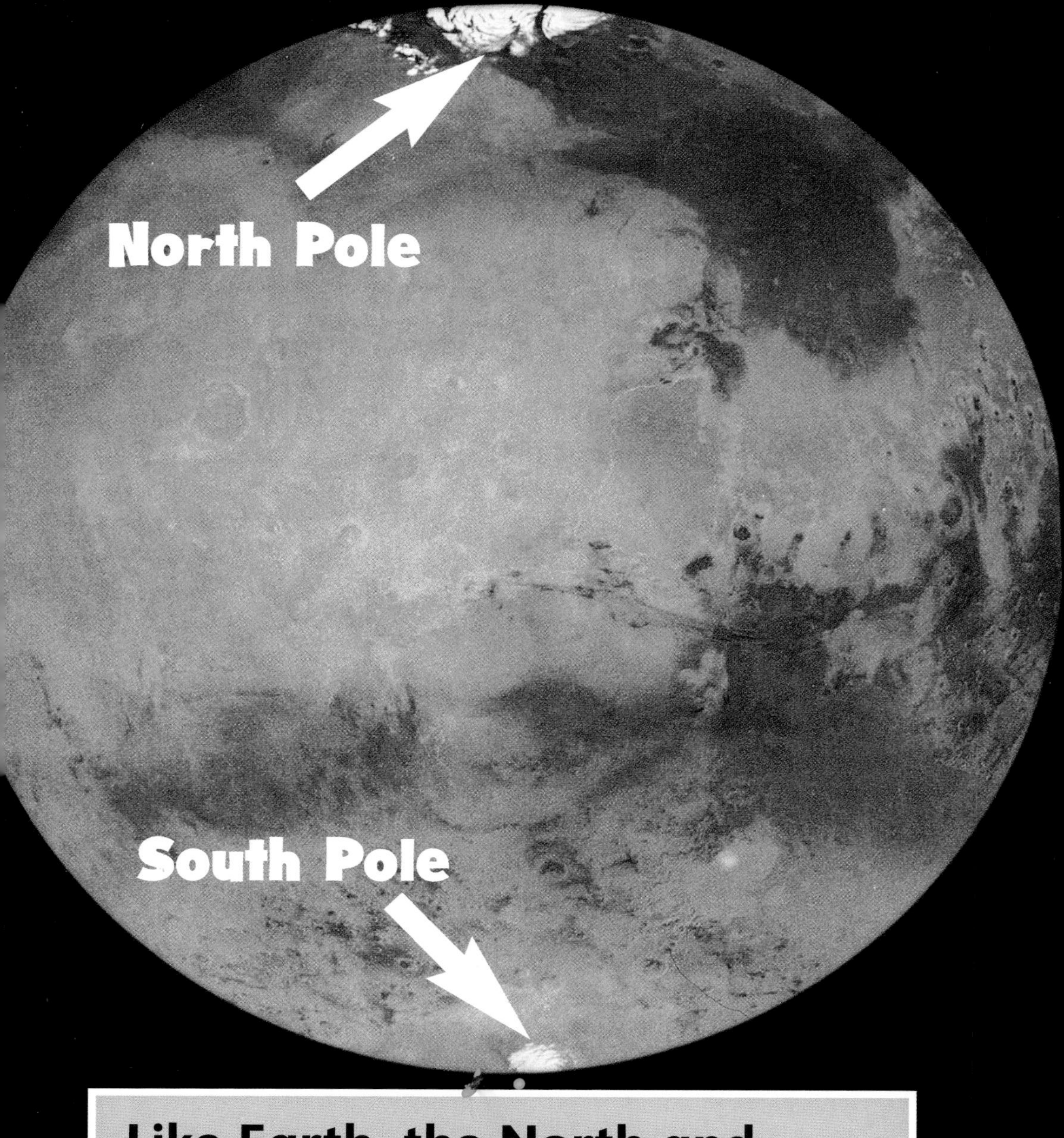

North Pole

South Pole

Like Earth, the North and South Poles on Mars have ice.

Mars is cold all the time.

Humans cannot breathe the air on Mars.

You would have to wear a **space suit** to breathe and stay warm on Mars.

EV2

Scientists are looking for signs of life on Mars.

They think people can live on Mars someday.

Do you want to live on Mars?

Is this what a city on Mars might look like?

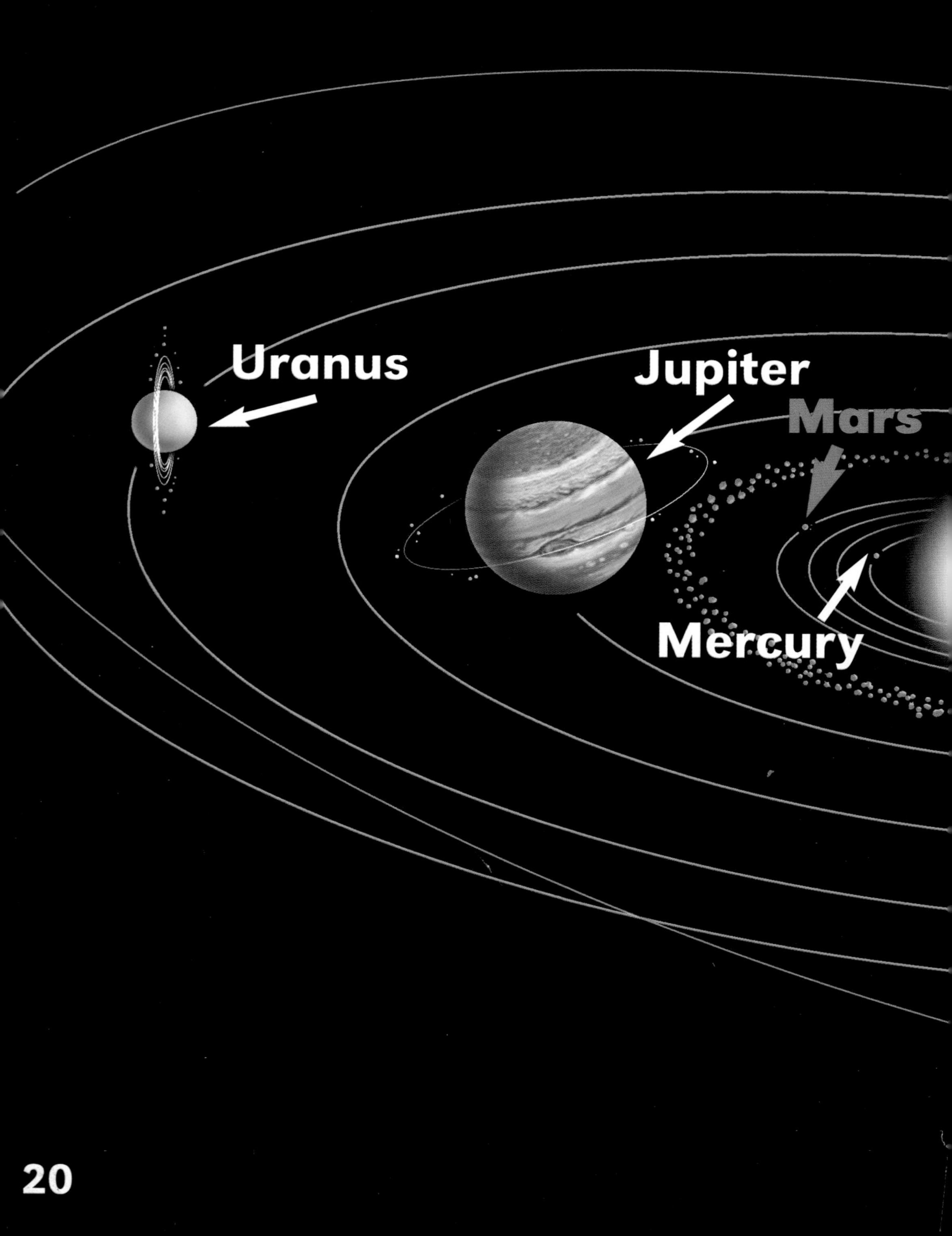
Uranus
Jupiter
Mars
Mercury

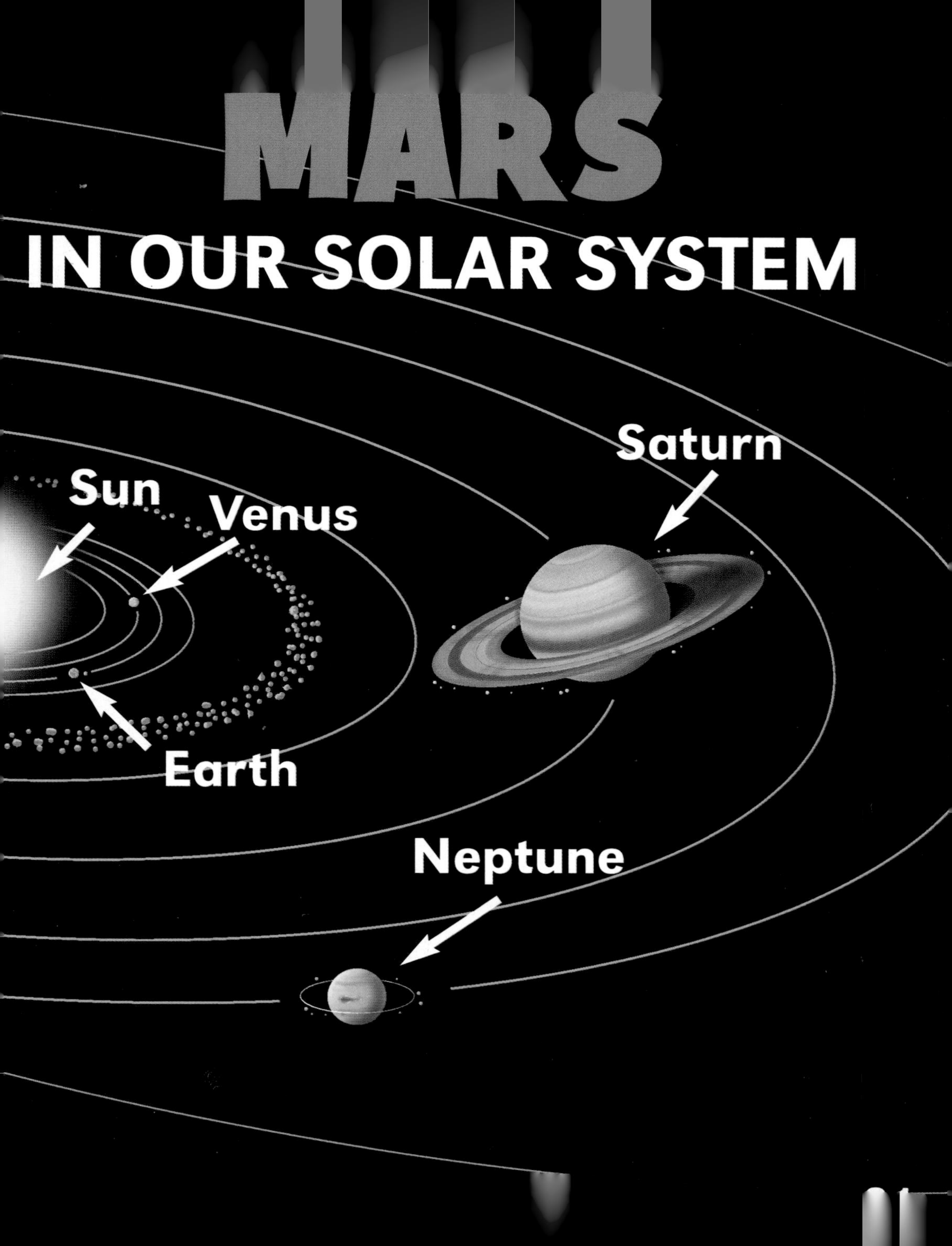
MARS
IN OUR SOLAR SYSTEM
Saturn
Sun
Venus
Earth
Neptune

YOUR NEW WORDS

astronaut (**ass**-truh-nawt) a person trained to travel in space

astronomer (uh-**stron**-uh-mur) someone who studies stars, planets, and space

Mars (mars) a planet named after the Roman god of war

rover (**roh**-ver) a robot used to explore the surface of a planet or moon

solar system (**soh**-lur **siss**-tuhm) the group of planets, moons, and other things that travel around the Sun

space suit (spayss soot) special clothing to wear in space

telescope (**tel**-uh-skope) a tool used to see things far away

Earth and Mars

A year is how long it takes a planet to go around the Sun.

1 Earth year
=365 days

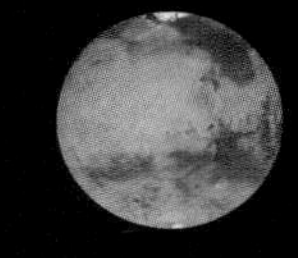
1 Mars year
=687 Earth days

A day is how long it takes a planet to turn one time.

1 Earth day
= 24 hours

1 Mars day
= 24–25 Earth hours

A moon is an object that circles a planet.

Earth has
1 moon.

Mars has
2 moons.

Olympus Mons, the biggest volcano on Mars, is 3 times as tall as Mount Everest.

INDEX

FIND OUT MORE

Book:

Stille, Darlene R. *Mars.* Mankato, MN: Child's World, 2003.

Web site:

Solar System Exploration
http://sse.jpl.nasa.gov/planets/

MEET THE AUTHOR

Melanie Chrismer grew up near NASA in Houston, Texas. She loves math and science and has written thirteen books for children. To write her books, she visited NASA where she floated in the zero-gravity trainer called the Vomit Comet. She says, "it is the best roller coaster ever!"